# POETS FOR PALESTINE

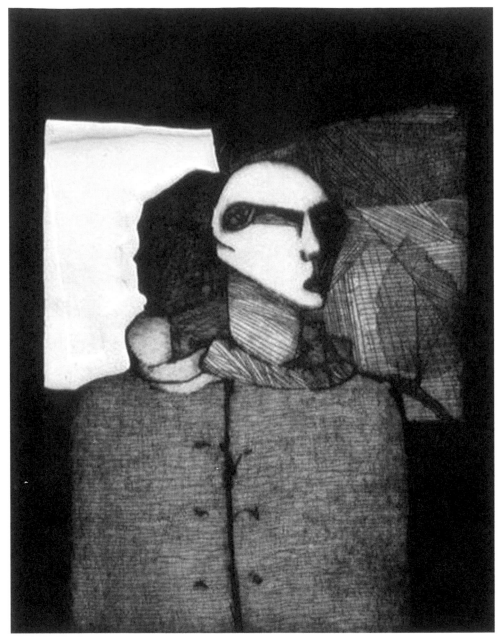

Nasser Soumi, *Mémoires Tristes*, 1979. Aquatint, 12.5″ × 10″

# POETS FOR PALESTINE

*Edited by Remi Kanazi*

Al Jisser Group, 2008

First published in 2008 by

Al Jisser Group
DBA A Gathering of the Tribes, Inc.
And its subsidiary Fly By Night Press
P.O. Box 255
New York, NY 10013
Email: Poets4Palestine@gmail.com

**Library of Congress Cataloging-in-Publication Data**
ISBN # 1-930083-09-2

Photography and captions provided by Samia A. Halaby
Design, typography, and production by Amani Semadi

FOR
THE PEOPLE
OF
PALESTINE

# Contents

Abdal Rahman Mozayen, *Children of the Intifada*, 1988. Ink on paper, 19.5″ × 25.5″

# Acknowledgements

This volume is the result of the collaborative efforts of many people, some of whose contributions were so great as to require special mention. Anyone interested in understanding the modern Palestinian experience will find an invaluable resource in Samia A. Halaby, a founder of Al Jisser, whose inspiration and insight were crucial to the creation of this anthology. The thirty pieces of art before you are the result of Halaby's efforts, whose curatorial eye was vital to the completion of this project. Also indispensable was Nathalie Handal, who first reached out to many of the poets whose work is contained here, and then shared her acute skills as a poet and editor to sharpen the vision of this book. Special thanks also go to Amani Semadi, who patiently and expertly laid out draft after draft of this collection. My deepest gratitude goes to Vinnie Gaetano, who provided inestimable editorial consultation during the final stages of this project. I owe a tremendous thanks to each of the translators, whose exceptional efforts greatly enhanced the quality of this volume. The poets and artists who contributed their work are, of course, the very fabric of this book. Each voice featured here is unselfish and unique. Their work illustrates the necessity for change and demonstrates reason for hope. On a personal note, whatever success my own efforts find is really the success of my parents, whom I do not often thank enough for the education and encouragement they continually provide.

Finally, a note about Al Jisser. Formed in 2001, Al Jisser ("the bridge") is a small group of New York artists and poets committed to focusing international attention on contemporary Arab art in all its social, economic, and political dimensions. Among its volunteer-driven projects have been *Williamsburg Bridges: Palestine 2002*, which showcased the work of fifty Palestinian artists at the Williamsburg Art and Historical Center, and *Palestine: Art of Resistance*, at Tribes Gallery in September 2003. Beginning in March 2006, over four thousand visitors experienced *Made in Palestine*, the first exhibition of contemporary Palestinian art featured in New York City. My deepest thanks go to Al Jisser for taking on this project and continuing to shine light on Arab artistry.

# Introduction

In 1948, my grandmother was expelled from Palestine. Like many of the 780,000 Palestinians evicted that year, she never saw her birthplace again. But she always dreamed of a dignified return: to Yaffa, her home city, a place of warmth and beauty; to her house, which, in her heart, towered higher than the hills of Lebanon; and to an unfettered life, which no apology or compensation could ever replace. My grandmother passed on her story to inspire and galvanize—to ensure that her children and grandchildren, and all those they encountered, would never forget Palestine.

My own journey toward self-recognition started when I began to look more broadly at the struggles of indigenous populations throughout the world. I realized that Palestinians were not so "other" after all; there exists a substantial "we" of peoples alienated from our own lands across the globe. This recognition—and the repudiation of an accepted status quo which attempts to legitimize our dispossession—led me to activism. The Palestinian narrative had become much more than the story of my family's suffering. Palestine had become my cause.

As I continued to shape my views on social justice, I drew upon numerous accounts of oppression, including horrifying narratives of the Holocaust and Jewish suffering. Most of my education was in Catholic schools, where courses, from religion to history, acknowledged the pain endured by the Jewish people. The basic appeal of justice, I began to understand, transcends designations such as Arab and Christian and black. It is a fundamentally, irreducibly *human* appeal. I am convinced that my own activism is often fueled, not by an internal strength, but by the passion and efforts of so many in the Latino-American, Asian-American, and African-American communities as well as the solidarity shared with many across the religious spectrum.

I believe this human appeal is the reason that sentiment towards the Palestinian cause is growing. Groups such as the U.S. Campaign to End the Israeli Occupation, Jews Against Zionism, Environmentalists for Palestine, Queers Undermining Israeli Terrorism, and numerous others rally, keep vigil, write, and perform to secure justice for a people who have been occupied for more than forty years and disenfranchised for even longer. The terms of discussion have slowly shifted from whether one is "pro-Palestinian" to whether one is "anti-occupation," "anti-oppression," and "pro-justice."

This coalescence of voices inspired *Poets For Palestine*. In piecing together this volume, I sought to unite a younger generation of poets, spoken word artists, and hip-hop artists with those who, for decades, have used their words to elevate the consciousness of humanity.

At the first *Poets For Palestine* meeting, a small group of Al Jisser members gathered to discuss the logistics of assembling a brief chapbook. Our initial proposal called for the compiling of works from two nights of poetry, the *Poetic Injustice Poetry Shows*, which were held during the showing of the *Made in Palestine* and *3 Arab Painters in New York* art exhibits at *The Bridge* gallery in New York City. But as we ventured further into the project, we found ourselves eyeing grander goals. Our call for poetry reached a multitude of countries. We received submissions from the Occupied Territories, the broader Arab world, Europe, Australia, and the United States. In our call for poetry, we chose not to limit the subject matter solely to the topic of Palestine, instead widening our scope to issues as varied as the ongoing occupation of Iraq and Afghanistan as well as poetry on the Sudan and Lebanon.

Another aim of this project is to provide a forum for contemporary Palestinian youth. The young people of Palestine will be the next generation to sustain the vibrancy of Palestinian culture; cultivating their talents and showcasing their work is therefore crucial.

Finally, this collection is enhanced by Palestinian art. Calling on a range of immensely talented artists living under Israeli occupation and throughout the Diaspora, we present thirty powerful images, each of which highlights a unique dimension of the Palestinian experience.

On a personal note, this project reflects my own conversation on Palestine. In compiling the works featured herein, I discovered a multitude of new voices, each of whom propelled me to further grasp the necessity of poetry and art as human expression. From Amiri

Baraka to Patricia Smith to the N.O.M.A.D.S., poetry, spoken word, and hip-hop are embodied in *Poets For Palestine*.

I can only hope that the poems and images included here strike a chord within each reader—tapping into the core of what makes us all alike—and affects each one as deeply as they have affected me. Their voices transcend the surface and genuinely lead us down a road of possibility, reshaping the landscape of humanity, for this I am certain.

—Remi Kanazi

New York, New York

May 2, 2008

# POETS FOR PALESTINE

Jumana Husseini, *Al Quds*, 1967. Oil on canvas, 60″ × 44″

Mahmoud Darwish

## Who Am I, Without Exile?


A stranger on the riverbank, like the river...water
binds me to your name. Nothing brings me back from my faraway
to my palm tree: not peace and not war. Nothing
makes me enter the gospels. Not
a thing...nothing sparkles from the shore of ebb
and flow between the Euphrates and the Nile. Nothing
makes me descend from the pharaoh's boats. Nothing
carries me or makes me carry an idea: not longing
and not promise. What will I do? What
will I do without exile, and a long night
that stares at the water?

Water
binds me
to your name...
Nothing takes me from the butterflies of my dreams
to my reality: not dust and not fire. What
will I do without roses from Samarkand? What
will I do in a theater that burnishes the singers with its lunar
stones? Our weight has become light like our houses
in the faraway winds. We have become two friends of the strange
creatures in the clouds...and we are now loosened
from the gravity of identity's land. What will we do...what
will we do without exile, and a long night
that stares at the water?

Water
binds me
to your name...
There's nothing left of me but you, and nothing left of you
but me, the stranger massaging his stranger's thigh: O
stranger! what will we do with what is left to us
of calm...and of a snooze between two myths?
And nothing carries us: not the road and not the house.
Was this road always like this, from the start,
or did our dreams find a mare on the hill
among the Mongol horses and exchange us for it?
And what will we do?
What

will we do
without
exile?

*Translated from the Arabic by Fady Joudah*

Bashar Hroub, *Crucified Woman*, 2004. Acrylic on paper, 11.75″ × 8.25″

Amiri Baraka

**Enemy of Civilization**


    **The Palestinians**
**call you "Enemy**
**Of the Sun,"** from a bunker
Barely able to see
The sky. But I
Here in the automatic
Dungeon of the Devil
Atop his slice of
Gold slobbering Evil
See what I see, &
It is not just The
Sun, the demon has
Declared teeth & claw
War, blood libel
No survival, They
It Them He from the
Loud canon of
Ignorant violence
Detest the idea of
Humanity. He It They
Them, call for the
Non-beginning the
Savage unbeing of
Anything that sees,
Hears, feels, is touched,
Can smell, anything that
Sings, anything, one, body,
Wants to create, not
Destroy or obliterate.
He It Them They have
Ruled history illegal
& the future a nutty
vision, the root of
all division, these
guys, dolls, gogs
Magogs, them heels
& charlatans, them
Heathens & beasts
& monsters & haints
those preposterous liars

truth deniers, Imbeciles
cannibals, omnivorous
criminals, dem wealthy
tramps, colossal
flesh eating ants,
them uncle and missile
Sams, them humiliated
losers in N Korea &
Viet Nam, has declared
Civilization treason
along with thought,
friendship & reason.
They, it them have
Said civilization &
Its provocateurs
Have got to be
Killed dead.
& further, said them
they it, beast, 666
proclaim those who
want to be human
insane.
          NO, not just
Enemies of The Sun
But enemies of life
& the world, enemies
of humanity, & of
Civilization itself.
These are Amoebas
Of the 21st century,
One celled poisonous
Organisms, aspiring
To become hyperbotulistic
Viruses of disease
Ridden Capitalism
Smears of epidemic
Racism. Gods
Of the bottom of
The toilet bowl.
The Devil was old
Fashioned they mumble
We ain't humble
The Devil was a
Do-Gooder &
Everybody know

Anything near good
is deadly. That
Is what the Enemies
Of Civilization
Say (when they ain't
Lying)

Nabil Anani, *Over the Wall*, 2004. Mixed media on paper, 27.5˝ × 19.5˝

Melissa Tuckey

## Portrait of Mona Lisa in Palestine

I.

Someone's been erasing her jawbone again
better she have no jaw at all
than a prominent chin

They say the sea's too restless
the horizon too full of promise

They've given her a drab background
and pocket of crushed cigarettes Taken
away her veranda—replaced

the valley with a prison courtyard
Laughter used to rise from her mouth like birds
Fish leapt at the sound of her voice

Now they paint her mouth closed
They can't stand
the way she looks at them

II.

*She shouldn't have left the house for water*

*She shouldn't have gone to school that day*

*She shouldn't let her kids play in front of the Mosque*

*She shouldn't have been standing
in front of that bulldozer*

*She shouldn't have so many children*

Curators worry the mask is cracking

Beneath it all kinds of things we wouldn't want to know

**III.**

She wears no jewels

The dictionary says that rape
is the pumice
of grapes a turnip
a forage crop for sheep

that rapture is rape
by God

that God is occupant
in a theater
and you can add "of war"
to any sentence

thunderbolt of war
maidenflowerhead of war

that war is a bowl of
chowder

heroics the opposite
of hysterics—

Ghassan Zaqtan

## The Camp Prostitute


What those intend who visit her house
Is palpably felt
So pure, so proud.

Those who stayed late in the fields
Will find her hanging near the little trees
The five mossy steps
Then the bougainvillea plant by the door.

Her bracelets jingling in their sleep like a phantom horse
Her undergarments coloring their dreams
Her breasts well trodden like the path to the mill
Her ritual movements between the bed and the wash basin
Like a popular song all the rage.

The still life on the wall
The sheets and two pillows
The scent of cheap cologne
The nails behind the door
Where the smell of their clothes still lingers
The jasmine outside the window

The numbed convolutions of her body
The strain pervading her silence

The intentions of those passing through to her house
The passersby and the visitors,
The students, clerks and chickens
The vans, the guards and the dogs,
The porters, the cats and the vegetable sellers
The fathers and sons
All those who have left their smell in her broken sleep
They were all of them there
Behind the kids
The cart
The coffin
So pure, on their way to her destination.


*Translated from the Arabic by May Jayyusi and Alan Brownjohn*

Mustafa Hallaj, *People Moving*, 1980. Masonite cut, 27.5″ × 40″

E. Ethelbert Miller

**Fathers in Exile**

We are exiles
Not only from the land but from our sons.
The young men who no longer desire our worn suitcases and torn books.

We never held
A map of love, a way of knowing
The secret directions to the heart.

When we became fathers
Something made us jump back from the heat of it,
The burning of innocence, the hot iron scars on our failed flesh.

It was about the land and body we could no longer see or touch.
Between the entrance and the exit.
Between somewhere and nowhere.

We tried to make a home out of the ruins of imagination.
What is lost is bone and memories more than sperm.
The faces of our sons are the fingerprints on our souls.

Our sons catch breath—struggle to breathe
Each small fist a nail hammered to air.

Abdal Rahman Mozayen, *Intifada: Against Fascism*, 1988. Ink on paper, 25.5″ × 20″

Remi Kanazi

## Palestinian Identity

I was born overseas
A refugee
With little knowledge of myself or my ancestry
Growing up in American society
I conformed to the mentality
I watched MTV
Envied actors and people who drove Mercedes
I didn't listen to Public Enemy or read Edward Said
Comprehend the need for autonomy
I was a dark kid, trying to be a white kid, acting like a black kid
In my middle-class economy
But my mom didn't speak this language perfectly
And I was reminded with certainty
My name wasn't Ali or Punjabi MC
Not Khalid, Rashid, or anyone from Aladdin's family
I was just me

But who was me?
I asked the question quietly
As my relatives suffered
Fighting oppression in Mideast countries
What is Palestinian identity?
What was preventing me from seeing what others
Pointed out so easily?
It's scary not having autonomy
The only one with a permanent tan on the baseball team
But it's funny being seen
I know, I look like the terrorist in that movie
Yup, the biggest nose in three counties
Yet I think I figured it out eventually
I'm a Palestinian-American
Standing proudly with one foot on democracy
And the other seeking autonomy
While the media tries to rewrite my people's history

I will always be me
With my roots planted firmly
American with Palestinian ancestry
Planting seeds for hybrid ideology
In lands of productivity

You see these schemes aren't just a dream
It's what I say, know, and mean
And one day the truth will be seen
With transparency
So I step forward
A part of a team
The true essence of what I believe to be
American Palestinian identity

Dima Hilal

## Ar-Rahman Road

On my street,
    mercy resides

Spiders get carried out of houses
in styrofoam cups
gently airlifted to safety

Children swap legos for tonka trucks for barbies
never chided for not sharing
broken toys buried in the backyard
    (along with hard feelings)

Housewives make pies
twenty at a time
cherry, strawberry, peach, pumpkin
deliver them to neighbors' doorsteps
disperse them in the park
freshly baked presents
next to sleeping bags and cardboard boxes

On my block church bells ring
early on Sunday morning
and every prayer is for another

The Lord's prayer mingles
with the sound of the *adhan*
floating from the nearby mosque

On my street
we want for nothing,
    but *salaam*

Long for nothing,
    just *rahman*

Sholeh Wolpé

**And So It Goes...**


In the dusty market beneath makeshift canopies,
bodies captive in Baghdad's summer heat,
she tugs on her mother's *chador*, holds up a copper coin
in her tiny palm, asks *where to buy bombs to attack the Americans.*

My child cousin often marched around the round
mahogany table, fist punching air, chanting:
*Marg bar Shah. Death to the Shah.*

Months later, the Shah fled Iran.

Drought-empowered beetles, hungry,
killed countless old pines in San Bernardino mountains.
                    Then came the fire,
                                ruthless, sweeping...

Vera Boulos Issa Omar, *Maze*, 2003. Crayons on card stock, 11.5″ × 9.25″

Ibtisam Barakat

**Curfew**


Our city is a cell
Children's faces
Are replacing
Flower pots on
Window sills.
And we are waiting.

From our bars
Of boredom
We enter
A spit race
The one whose spit
Reaches farther
Is freer.

We look to the sky
Squint our questions.

We turn the sun
Into a kite
Hold it with a ray
Till it is torn up
Inside the horizon.

And the light is
Peeled off the ground
A page in a bedtime story
We do not understand.

Our questions remain
A yeast
Inside our chests,
Rising.

Philip Metres

## Installation/Occupation

*after Vera Tamari in Ramallah*

**1.**

there was a time you couldn't paint     red white
green or black     could be a flag     imagine

you couldn't paint poppies or watermelon
now you can paint all you want     & yet this state

of uncertainty     will the doors hold out
can you leave your house can you walk around

this occupation     when the tanks come
crack down     drive the sidewalks for fun     for weeks

all these smashed cars lining the city streets
my friend's red Beetle     flipped over     its legs in the air

so in a field     we paved a road to nowhere     & placed
the crushed     in a column     as if in a rush hour

line of traffic     we had an opening     at our piece
a huge party on our road     & then walked home

**2.**

before dawn a column of Merkavas
came back     my house was opposite the field

& I could see the tanks pull up     & yield
two heads emerged from turrets     trying to read

the scene     then went back inside the hatch
& ran over the exhibit     over & over

again backwards and forwards     then shelled it
& for good measure christened it with piss

I caught it all on video     this metamorphosis
of the piece     there's the story of Duchamp

once the workmen installing his exhibit
dropped a crate of paintings     the floor

shattering the glass     Duchamp ran over
thrilled     now he said     now it is complete

Vénus Khoury-Ghata

## FROM **The Seven Honeysuckle-sprigs of Wisdom**

Roads which cross other people's dreams lead nowhere
says Massouda the wise woman while blowing into the stem of her
    *narguileh*
Her smoke-rings make the canary dizzy; he suspects the earth of
    speeding up its rotation to reach night more quickly, night which
    fades his mistress' beauty

Massouda's cards never lie
Three aces followed by three jacks mean a plague of locusts
A change of mayor is inevitable when three kings line up on the table
Massouda's counsels are listened to by the archbishop whose Mass she
    prompts by making her bench creak

Khalid who made a fortune selling oats buttons up his fly on his marble
    balcony within sight of his mare
She recognizes him by the odor of his sweat and by his whip which
    lashes the clouds during droughts to make them rain on his field

*Translated from the French by Marilyn Hacker*

Rima Mozayen, *Three Women*, 1999. Mixed media on paper, 27.5˝ × 19.5˝

Kathy Engel

**Untitled**


I am the Palestinian woman,
the Israeli woman.
We are cousins.
How do I imagine—
memory
holding history
too harsh to taste,
how do I speak my language
invent a new one
each syllable a volcano
reconfiguring the earth.
If I say what I know
will you still listen?
And can I still live in my body then?
How do I imagine
my two hearts, one belly
voice of blood—
a just geography
in this place
in this year
start here:
say words: home, olive, name
city, earth, language
coffee, wine, water
school, work, travel
no passbook id card
imagine:
we can acknowledge
pause
a moment without fear
I can't say everything.
No woman can.
My hips carry sticks for fire
burnt villages, secrets,
shards of bulldozed homes,
poems,
children
and their dreams.

All things are not the same
that's all I can say, today
in this place.
But I am here to imagine.

Laila Halaby

**a moonlit visit**


*for Bari*

up before dawn
I peek out at the full yellow moon
read a page or two for inspiration
glance at the author's picture...

your eyes stare back
sitting across from me in my quiet house
your long fingers resting on my table
you gaze at me through soft brown eyes

more than twenty years has passed
since your lanky east
stretched out on the green lawn
of our Midwestern college

though we were close in age
I was younger, innocent, optimistic
never a heroin user or abused child
I was your clean self
and you often made me cry
on your way to becoming my best friend
confidante in all matters
my other half
but never my boyfriend
in the American sense of the word

we (you much more than I)
led double lives then
West and East
drinking, sex, and parties
with them
politics, stories, nighttime walks
with each other

fingers entwined
we walked in the rain
up the steps of a cathedral
swapping tales of moons and lovers

made them ours
while my feet bled
through white sneakers
while you fiddled
with the heavy silver ring you always wore
God's message scribbled across it
(for years it amazed me
that for all your drinking
you never lost that ring
God never forsook you)

it took three years of walks and talks
of lying together as one
for you to tell me you loved me
eastern style
like in folktales
even as you loved woman after woman
western style
like in movies
had sex with that tall blond girl
behind the bushes by the dorms
locked yourself up for days
with the giggly Jewish girl
who went through several Pakistani boyfriends
but when I arrived early for a visit
you wouldn't open the door for me
until you had put on a shirt
would not let me walk alone
to a friend's house in early evening

eastern love in the west
even the Midwest
is tiresome, more so when it reeks of liquor
cruelty and suicide threats
how many times
did I empty your glass
take you home
tuck you in to sleep off your self loathing?
how many times
did I listen
as you plotted out
your own death?
still too innocent
to understand that some things
cannot be undone

or fixed

it took years to break free
untangle myself from
your knots and snarls
shake off those long fingers
that held me just barely above the surface

the moon this morning
your eyes in that novelist's face
seeing you sitting at my table
I missed you terribly
went searching for you in cyberspace
but there were only wispy traces

are you dead
or back in Pakistan
or in Las Vegas or Texas
with an American wife
or sleeping with men
or sticking needles in your arm
as you did once
long ago

or have you
always been here
with me
my other self

my lost majnoon

Mustafa Hallaj, *Battle of Karameh*, 1969. Masonite cut, 12˝ × 16.5˝

Ghassan Zaqtan

**Black Horses**


The slain enemy
Think of me without mercy in their eternal sleep
Ghosts ascend the stairways of the house, rounding the corners
The ghosts I picked up from the roads
Collecting them from the sins around other people's necks.

The sin hangs at the throat like a burden
It is there I nurture my ghosts and feed them
The ghosts that float like black horses in my dreams.

With the vigor of the dead the latest Blues song rises
While I reflect on jealousy
The door is warped open, breath seeps through the cracks
The breath of the river
The breath of drunkards, the breath
Of the woman who awakes to her past in a public park.

When I sleep
    I see a horse grazing the grass
When I fall asleep,
    The horse watches over my dreams

On my table in Ramallah
There are unfinished letters
And pictures of old friends
The manuscript of a young poet from Gaza
An hourglass
And opening lines that flap in my head like wings.

I want to memorize you like that song in first grade
The one I hold onto
Complete and
With no mistakes
The lisp, the tilt of the head, off key
The small feet pounding the concrete so eagerly
The open palms pounding the benches.

They all died in the war
My friends and classmates
Their little feet

Their eager little hands...they still pound the floors of each room
They pound the tables;
And still pound the pavements, the backs of the passersby,
Their shoulders.
Wherever I go
I see them
I hear them.

*Translated from the Arabic by May Jayyusi and Alan Brownjohn*

Nasri Zacharia, *Day of the Martyr*, 1996. Ballpoint on card stock, 15″ × 20″

# The N.O.M.A.D.S.

## Moot

*Omar Offendum*

Where peace had once flourished
All I can see is suffering
My cousins are malnourished
Their land taken for "buffering"
Uttering a cry for help is pretty useless
When people view your whole existence as useless
Ruthless...dictators misrepresenting
Signing your life away without your consenting
Skepticism & pessimism's all I feel
When nepotism & Zionism won't yield
Belittling soldiers are riddling shoulders & backs
With the marks of oppression as was done to blacks
And Native Americans who have vanished from sight
Maybe that's why "whites" don't understand why we fight
I'm seeing rights being stripped more than cars in the ghetto
But folks like us are like dust that won't settle
The thorn in your side that will move with the tide
And has never had any reason to hide so we ride...
Out in the open in broad daylight
Rocks in fists ready to topple these regimes despite
Odds that would have made the average poker player think twice
And we've proven that we ain't no mice
Still sometimes I'm feeling like a lab rat
The type that scientists like to take stabs at
The type that Zionists love to give bad reps
Claiming we're terrorists that are "mad strapped"
Like bagged crack—we move from our hoods
To the Jews'
Yaffa to Tel Aviv to the televised news
They see us as suicidal & under suspicion
Or could we be some freedom fighters on a mission
Itching for some Paradise...Now?

*Mr. Tibbz (Israeli Soldier)*

I tried my hardest to be patient,
But how they gonna cause violence without reciprocation?

They're fighting for a long lost nation
And I don't care about their problems or their present situation.
I hate them,
Be them Muslim or Arab.
The bastards shot my bride-to-be the day before my marriage.
So I'm doing this for Tara,
Because If I do none, then them punks won
And that's another win for terror.
I wouldn't dare give them the pleasure.
I wish I had a Kalashnikov so I could let off some pressure.
Run in the mosque during Fajr,
And split them bastards wide open like a secretary does a letter.
It's never enough, we give them land they want more.
They must be nuts, we give them peace they want war.
They're nothing but animals crawling round on all fours,
So when they attack we react with armed force.
It's hardcore.
The losses are preposterous.
I thought if I enlisted maybe I can help to stop this.
But I see now just how foul it gets,
The first day the drill sergeant told us cadets, he said
"The Arabs are your enemy, Palestinians especially,
And wiping them all out—that's the safest remedy."
That's what they keep telling me
But I ain't that way.
So I'ma chill at this East Tel Aviv café.


*Mr. Tibbz (Freedom Fighter)*

Never had a home.
My country wasn't mine.
I heard the propaganda about a hundred times.
Not a day passed, without my mother crying.
They shot the protesters, that's more brothers dying.
I'm trying hard to rise above it,
But it's really hard to work for something
When your life's full of nothing.
It's rough and tough in this holy land turned damned.
No education, born and raised in concentration camps.
Or crowd containment camps as it's called by the Zionists,
But we all know a Zionist is nothing but a lying bitch.
I could've been a doctor; I could've been a scientist
Instead they got me sinning selling broke kitchen appliances.
I'm tired of this, everyday my living gets harder.

Raised by my mother 'cause I never knew my father,
They shot him and my brother in the first intifada
And all they did was walk into the wrong part of Gaza.
Fuck the Jews, Americans too.
All they do is shoot us up then brag about it on the news.
They call us enemies of peace, well who's shooting who?
The UN can't help; they act like they ain't got a clue.
Yassir who? Arafat crap!!!
Man that cat talks smack but he don't deliver jack shit.
That's it; I can't let it come to pass.
I'm gonna make a change and so I'm siding with Hamas.
Three day fast, by the fourth got what I need.
By 9:30 I'm on the streets of East Tel Aviv.
Final prayer to god "A-yo Allah help me please,
I didn't want to kill but Israel won't let me be."
Count to three—take my last steps.
Get in the café—take my last breath.
Set off the detonator—big blast effect.
My life was pure hell so in death I rest.

Zuhdie Adawi, *Day of the Prisoner*, 1984. Crayons on cloth, 17˝ × 12˝

Hamida Begum

**The Promised Land**


My home isn't my own you say
That it never belonged to me
Even my land isn't my own you said
It was promised to you by God

But how can you take our home from us?
Why can we not share?
And why do you say you're the chosen?
For us God does not care?

Does God not want Ibrahim here?
My brother who's only two
And I know sometimes I misbehave
But doesn't God want me here too?

Though you believe it's your promised land
Let's all share without fear
And I know for sure
It's sure, I'm sure
That God does want us here!

Tahani Salah

**Hate**


I have this image in my head that one day when I step off this airplane
I'll be on this land where the air is sweeter than any fruit I have tasted
And that the land is softer than any cloud I could ever imagine
And that peace was possible
But for now the mothers of our holy land
are being stabbed raped and murdered
And before I can get to her she has fallen
My siblings and I feel guilty that we haven't given her ourselves
For we bleed her blood
For her blood runs through me
I speak for her will and for people
even though there's no one to listen anymore
Still your question stands
Why do these Palestinian children hate so much?
It shouldn't be why it should be what kind of hate do they have?
Because it was never for a people nor a cause
This hate keeps them alive
This hate makes them live another day even though there's nothing to
live for
This hate puts air in their lungs even though there might not be tomorrow
This hate makes them want to have children just to teach them not to hate
Because on the other side hate is grown through children
Hate is grown through trees in the shape of a V never for peace
For their own protection
Hate is shown through black sheets of separation never integration
Hate is the fact that in this country we teach our six-year-olds to step
and throw baseballs in little league games with crowds of parents
cheering behind them
And in other countries there are six-year-old children step and throw
rocks to protect the tears and lives of their grandparents that anguish
had caused
So maybe this hate is not your ordinary hate
Maybe this hate kept my father alive
Maybe this hate makes children feel as if they have to hold their shit in
one extra day just to feel full

So before you could ever say you didn't mean it that way six-year-old
children walking downs roads kicking pebbles the wrong way get shot at
Seven-year-old children walking down roads speaking the wrong
language at the wrong time get shot at

And before you could ever say you were sorry the mothers of our holy
land are being stabbed raped and murdered
And before you could ever learn of her or I could ever get to her
she has fallen

Saed Hilmi, *Untitled*, 1993. Acrylic on canvas, 39˝ × 27.5˝

Nathalie Handal

**Wall Against Our Breath**


Everyday a crueler hour—
     the fencing of hearts barely beating,
the palpitation of leaves in our dry gardens
     the heat in Gaza in Jericho
keeping dreams we never had the time to remember
     an old woman trying to revive
any fantasy she can, another
     thinking of her husband
lost nowhere she can imagine—
     men over barbed wire who stop
answering when we scream their name
     too busy—trying to cross the checkpoint,
the soldiers the day the night
     while others drink tea, talk about curfews
women, the children they buried
     while a mother asks
what she will tell the child inside her
     *that she wish it did not come*

We witness October in flames,
     and every other month following,
is the same, the streets
     we walk through a reminder
of who we are and what they will
     never make of us...
human portraits in corners
     we forget to look at or forget to reach...
pictures stuck on walls as if
     they belong nowhere
a groom and bride forced to wed
     anywhere but where they should,
and yet, we keep asking:
     what victory blows candles out
what sea speaks of another sea

Even if they raise the wall higher
     than we can reach
we know only one home
     even if we take different routes each time
the trees guide us the wind guides us

the sun and the moon guide us
and when we arrive we find the books
        we cannot stop reading, the embroideries
the refugees made, the kitchen
        where our lives were lived—
a marriage proposal a death a birth—
        and everyday as we brew our coffee
we greet each other properly
        and chase the wall from our breath

Deema Shehabi

**Lights Across the Dead Sea**

Where were we
if not at the beginning?
The wind ambled
off the salt water,
the distance fractured
our gaze without a blink,
and the moon rushed
into the dark rouge of the hills.
*Imagine*, I said, *if those hills
were still ours*.
But you had already counted
the bone bites
of a lost country,
opened each page
of those wounds to full glow.

The calm was too far off
to be remembered—
All around us: leftover
stones, look-alike
orchards full of lemons
and guavas,
white bolts of bandaged
children—
morning still trembling
on their lips,
their grassy lashes glaring
across makeshift coffins:
why do we carry
those children in the blur

of the moon's afterglow?
*But at least they lived
and fought on their land*, I said
recalling our last return—
was it the last?
when my mother soured
the soldier's eyes
with her talk of blood
and the laws of its searing.

Then she loosened
her forehead and said:
"*Look closely and you will still
see the etch of sweet sap
that comes from loving your land.*"

But you crimped your breath
and held it in your mouth,
your eyes embering darkly.
*Listen*, I told you,
*this affection is not a failure*,
while the lights across the Dead Sea
unsheathed
but betrayed nothing.

Adnan Yahya, *Sabra and Shatila*, 1983. Ink on paper, 21.5″ × 24.5″

Lisa Suhair Majaj

## The Coffin Maker Speaks

At first it was shocking—orders flooding in
faster than I could meet. I worked
through the nights, tried to ignore
the sound of planes overhead,
reverberations shaking my bones,
acid fear, the jagged weeping
of those who came to plead my services.
I focused on the saw in my hands,
burn of blisters, sweet smell of sawdust;
hoped that fatigue would push aside
my labor's purpose.

Wood fell scarce as the pile of coffins grew.
I sent my oldest son to scavenge more,
but there was scant passage on the bombed out roads.
And those who could made it through
brought food for the living, not planks for the dead.
So I economized, cut more carefully than ever,
reworked the extra scraps.
It helped that so many coffins were child-sized.

I built the boxes well, nailed them strong,
loaded them on the waiting trucks,
did my job but could do no more.
When they urged me to the gravesite—
that long grieving gash in earth
echoing the sky's torn warplane wound—
I turned away, busied myself with my tools.
Let others lay the shrouded forms in new-cut wood,
lower the lidded boxes one by one:
stilled row of toppled dominos,
long line of broken teeth.
Let those who can bear it read the Fatiha
over the crushed and broken dead.
If I am to go on making coffins,
let me sleep without knowledge.

But what sleep have we in this flattened city?
My neighbors hung white flags on their cars
as they fled. Now they lie still and cold,

waiting to occupy my boxes.
Tonight I'll pull the white sheet
from my window.
Better to save it for my shroud.

One day, insha'allah, I'll return
to woodwork for the living.
I'll build doors for every home in town,
smooth and strong and solid,
that will open quickly in times of danger,
let the desperate in for shelter.
I'll use oak, cherry, anything but pine.

For now, I do my work. Come to me
and I'll build you what you need.
Tell me the dimensions, the height or weight,
and I'll meet your specifications.
But keep the names and ages to yourself.
Already my dreams are jagged.
Let me not wake splintered from my sleep
crying for Fatima, Rafik, Soha, Hassan, Dalia,
or smoothing a newborn newdead infant's face.
Later I too will weep. But if you wish me
to house the homeless dead,
let me keep my nightmares nameless.

*South Lebanon, 2006*

Sholeh Wolpé

## Morning After the U.S. Invasion of Iraq

It is as it has always been.
At Starbucks across from Disneyland

People suck coffee from paper cups,
munch on muffins, bagels and cakes.

The chatter is as always, excited.
The smiles as always, broad.

But today the sun is concealed and the breeze
brings no news of the blooming trees inside the park.

Perhaps last night trees shed blossoms like sap
—trees grieve like that.

Hayan Charara

## The Price of Tomatoes

The cardboard sign reads
"$1.99 each."

Granted, they're blood red,
firm, smell like my mother's garden.

Yet I cannot figure out
the price of these tomatoes.

I hold one up
under the long fluorescent bulbs

and remember the afternoon
when my mother, pruning

vines while on her knees
in the dirt, received news from Lebanon

about her father's shrinking stomach.
Plucked, left in the sun,

the fruits burst, their seeds
festered on the cracked earth

like tiny cancers.
"Israeli tomatoes,"

the grocer explains.
I leave the bag on the counter.

My grandfather, whose stomach
shrank to almost nothing,

smaller than a clenched fist,
wanted only clean water,

but the soldier,
who spoke Hebrew and Arabic,

refused. Instead,
he washes his shoes,

which were dirty, same as these
bright, shiny tomatoes

that cost so much.

Samia A. Halaby, *Ninth Wave of the Kafr Qasem Massacre: Embrace in Death*, 1999.
Pencil on paper, 9.5″ × 13″

Melissa Hotchkiss

**Regret**


I exhaust my body for apology
Where is my safe house?
Where is the elephant iris?
Last planted midsummer

Where is my safe house?
Near the hickory and larch trees
Last planted midsummer
My hair transformed as pine needles

Near the hickory and larch trees
A friend's death, irreconcilable
My hair transformed as pine needles
For evening entertainment Plains Indians

Often lit fir trees on fire
Where is my elephant iris?
A horizon intoxicates a body
I exhaust for apology

Veronica Golos

**Cain**


See the white ship.

The crossed swords with which I was made.
See the bow I have become, the bones, the arrow.

I became man, but not a man.

My past washes back, a low tide,
A haunting song.

Like the *zing* of the arrow—
Sound has a shape.

O flesh. There will be war.

Witness. Stand on the field
As the ones who are already dead

Need you to. Stare. Never let go.

One can not measure
Death.

I know. I am the one who cuts—broken
As the edge of your cup.

I will break the heart of my mother
To save this world.

Burhan Karkutly, *Yes to Palestine*, 1982. Ink on paper

Junichi P. Semitsu

**Palestine in Athens**


For opening ceremonies
I want athletes from Palestine in line
between those from Pakistan & Panama
waiting to enter the gates of the Coliseum
the only security checkpoint they know

I want Muhammad Ali to light
the Olympic torch & burn
every security fence in Gaza Strip

I want Bela Karolyi to carry
the next Keri Strug from Nabulus
the first Palestinian girl to need crutches
for reasons unrelated to war

I want every government
that ignored UN Resolution 242
to watch that red black green & white flag
rise so many times
they can't help humming the Anthem of the Intifada

I want the Flo-Jo of Jenin
sporting a hijab on a box of Wheaties
a hockey team sporting kuffiyehs
on the cover of Sports Illustrated
& Teen People pre-occupied with pole vaulters
from a post-occupied Palestine

I want Yassir Arafat to look into luge

I want airport security to suspect every Palestinian
of being a world record holder
& march them through gold medal detectors

I want to watch the Jesse Owens of Jerusalem
leave more smoke than a M203 grenade
the Randy Barnes of Bethlehem
fire shot puts farther than forty F16 missiles
the Marion Jones of Jericho
jump hurdles the height of 100 apartheid walls

for total Palestinian track & field domination
bringing home so much gold
the West Bank becomes the Bank of the West
& Fort Knox gets jealous

So let the Games begin
when the occupation ends
because I want the Olympic congregation
to recognize a nation
named
Palestine

Mohammad Wahibi, *Untitled*, 2003. Mixed media scratch board, 24″ × 20″

J. A. Miller

## Saudi Israelia

*Bart, having sex on prom night is as*
*American as our fifty-first state, Saudi Israelia!*
—Bart Simpson's girlfriend, Fox Network

Saudi Israelia, Saudi Israelia
Stronger, more potent than even Australia
Writers of Simpsons doth dreamt up that quip
Conscious or not, a great Freudian slip

Accurate too, long allies in secret
Cartoonish veracity which they won't admit
True character of twin theocracies
A perfect alliance, they match to a tee

Taliban to the left and the right of us too
Fundies each one, Wahhabi and Jew
(Don't forget Christians, they're in on the game
"The devil is secular!" they wail and complain)

Tel Aviv and Riyadh, then on to DC
Mono-theocracies fill them with glee
A figment you say, for laughs that are cheap?
Sorry to say folks, read 'em and weep

Published then perished long ago in Beirut
Documents surfaced their content acute
A green light was flashed from the House of Sa'ud
Straight to the Zios (the Arabs got screwed)

"Yallah!" cried Faisal, "Feel free! Go ahead!"
"Take Gaza! The West Bank! Fill Nasser with dread!"
A war will secure the oil trove for me
As well as my family (and also DC)

You'll get the land and we'll get the oil
Progressive forces thus completely embroiled
Those Palestinians? A troublesome crew
Leftist and secular they must be subdued

Printed quite plainly in black and in white
Faisal gave Eshkol an eager green light
Just for one day published there in full view
The next day—poof—gone! The subject taboo

But we all got the picture, the hand in the glove
Israel and Saudi a deep, secret love
How sweetly Abdullah held hands with the Prez
(Sharon wished he were there to add his caress)

Tripartite alliance of monotheists
Beating back justice with their bloody fists
A cartoon on Fox Network, ironic forsooth!
Bart's prescient prom date has blurted the truth

Hayan Charara

**Hamza Aweiwi, a Shoemaker in Hebron**

The taps have not been running
since July seventeenth,
his wedding day.
Now it's twenty-nine days
without clean water.

He has tanks on the roof.
Some days he manages to shave,
or his wife prepares the tea kettle.
But he knows the price of water.
It's holy, hard to come by.

Outside the shop, fat and bald,
an electrician with seven children
admits he does not wash his clothes.
A young girl, a yellow ribbon
in her hair, is laughing.
She knows grown men
should not smell this way.

He yanks a nail from a shoe
that needs to be resoled.
He knows he wouldn't need to fix them
to walk as far as where people live differently.
There, boys are washing cars,
housewives water lawns.

He seems troubled, hesitant,
looking for something in the distance,
but a cluster of trees
blocks the view.
He still daydreams
about taking long showers,
or even two a day.
But it's almost noon,
the temperature unbearable.
And the shoes are piling up.

Adnan Zbeidi, *A Rose is a Rose is a Banner*, 1998. Watercolor on paper, 27.5˝ × 19.5˝

Patricia Smith

## Humming When We Find Her

Lizzy Nkosi is. The song sounds strangely
familiar, a Glenn Miller riff in the midst of this.
Christ crucified crooked in one room
of the one-room house, Lizzy or somebody scrawl
*The Lord Is My Shepard* in careful block letters
beneath his impossibly square pink face.
There are
four chairs,
two tables,
one bed,
one bureau,
a plastic rendering of the Last Supper (Judas toppled,
wide-eyed),
a refrigerator thick with bird magnets,
a peeling ANC sticker,
a tarnished silver cross (Christ absent this time),
nine television sets in Lizzy's room.
*My husband, he fixes them.*
*Or is it they fix him?*

Lizzy, shot 11 times, is on crutches.
Smiling a wayward tooth,
she counts six bullets still in her chest,
dutifully angled away from the heart,
one still painfully lodged in the pit
of her arm. Fragments pepper
her hands, her skinny legs.
The scars look fresh and Lizzy's still counting,
this time her blessings.
*The last bullet hit a rand coin I had stuffed in my bra.*
She pauses so that we may feel
Death's presence, know for sure
that He is leaning against the refrigerator,
admiring the birds, setting Judas upright.

Lizzy's boy Bafana clings to her right crutch
and rides, and even though he is eight, too big,
she carries him.
*I know so many people*
*who are worse off than I am,*

*people who have no rooms at all.*
*My husband is good with his hands,*
*he finds work close to home.*
*My children are with me*
*and I pray that they are never hungry.*

Lizzy looks down at the crutches
that brace her withered legs.
*Oh, this?,* she says, as if just
discovering the damage.
*This is South Africa. This just happens.*

This just happens. These bright scars,
these simple losses, they have learned
to live with them, to pay them homage
and burn spices for their lives.
They knead them into the landscape,
these scars, these guests for supper.
They swallow them like bread,
feel them strengthen the walls of their bodies.
*This just happens.*
And happens. And happens.
They survive on the sharp meat of gunfire,
on land that refuses to grow anything but older.
What makes the ghost of Lizzy? The urge to
tense the smile,
make music out of cry
and wait for something else
to happen.

Ibtisam Barakat

## War Layers


Fear sits still on our tile,
A water carpet.
War vows, morning news
Fall like rocks into our days
And make the water rise.

Then fear swallows us,
Our footsteps, our beds, our food,
It raises a wet hand
To our books on the shelves.
It drinks the lines, the ink
Licks the pages blank,
And leaves.

At night I lay still wanting to steal
To myself an hour of fantasy
Soft, orange, round like the moon
That someday I would not sleep
Wearing the wet layers of war.

But outside,
The sounds of gunshots
Scatter as hail.
And inside, on the tile,
The stained minutes
Are knocked off teeth
From a smile.

Marian Haddad

## Making Arabic Coffee

The dark brown liquid, almost black,
the color of hickory, bubbling up. I
lift up this small pot as water rises.

Foam. Heat. Steam. I lift it away
from the fire, until it settles
down again. Let it boil once

more. Lift up—the same up
and down bobbing above the fire,
until the foam no longer rises.

The water has taken in
the flavor, color, taste
of our ground coffee beans,

and I remember quickly, the words
in Arabic; my mother warned,
*Latt Khaleeya't Foorr. Foorr.*

To overflow. To rise up.
To foam. Still, I cannot find
the English translation to suffice.

I had not remembered this
one Arabic word, *foorr*, until
memory rose up like the water

I color into coffee; the moment
brought me back to that place,
over the stove with my mother;

her behind me warning,
*Latt khaleeya't foorr.*
*Ay, haykee.* Yes, like this.

And so she taught me not to let
things overflow; and so she taught me
the way things rise.

Suleiman Mansour, *Last Supper*, 1986. Oil on canvas, 43″ × 51″

Naomi Shihab Nye

## My Father and the Figtree

For other fruits my father was indifferent.
He'd point at the cherry trees and say,
"See those? I wish they were figs."
In the evenings he sat my bed
weaving folktales like vivid little scarves.
They always involved a figtree.
Even when it didn't fit, he'd stick it in.
Once Joha was walking down the road and he saw a figtree.
Or, he tied his camel to a figtree and went to sleep.
Or, later when they caught and arrested him,
his pockets were full of figs.

At age six I ate a dried fig and shrugged.
"That's not what I'm talking about!" he said,
"I'm talking about a fig straight from the earth—
gift of Allah!—on a branch so heavy it touches the ground.
I'm talking about picking the largest fattest sweetest fig
in the world and putting it in my mouth."
(Here he'd stop and close his eyes.)

Years passed, we lived in many houses, none had figtrees.
We had lima beans, zucchini, parsley, beets.
"Plant one!" my mother said, but my father never did.
He tended garden half-heartedly, forgot to water,
let the okra get too big.
"What a dreamer he is. Look how many things he starts
and doesn't finish."

The last time he moved, I got a phone call.
My father, in Arabic, chanting a song I'd never heard.
"What's that?"
"Wait till you see!"
He took me out to the new yard.
There, in the middle of Dallas, Texas,
a tree with the largest, fattest, sweetest fig in the world.
"It's a figtree song!" he said,
plucking his fruits like ripe tokens,
emblems, assurance
of a world that was always his own.

Fady Joudah

**The Tea and Sage Poem**

At a desk made of glass,
In a glass walled-room
With red airport carpet,

An officer asked
My father for fingerprints,
And my father refused,

So another offered him tea
And he sipped it. The teacup
Template for fingerprints.

My father says, it was just
Hot water with a bag.
My father says, in his country,

Because the earth knows
The scent of history,
It gave the people sage.

I like my tea with sage
From my mother's garden,
Next to the snapdragons

She calls fishmouths
Coming out for air. A remedy
For stomach pains she keeps

In the kitchen where
She always sings.
First, she is Hagar

Boiling water
Where tea is loosened.
Then she drops

In it a pinch of sage
And lets it sit a while.
She tells a story:

The groom arrives late
To his wedding
Wearing only one shoe.

The bride asks him
About the shoe. He tells her
He lost it while jumping

Over a house-wall,
Breaking away from soldiers.
She asks:

Tea with sage
Or tea with mint?

With sage, he says.
Sweet scent, bitter tongue.
She makes it, he drinks.

Philip Metres

## Letter to My Sister

Katherine, when you came back
to our oak and maple suburb,
unreal, occupied, you caressed an olive tree
pendant, talked of ancestral homes

bulldozed for settler roads, olive groves
torn from the ground, your Palestinian love
unable to leave, his passport denied
at the airport. He'd never tell what he did

to be detained, words that could be taken
against your will. Instead, he gave you
this olive tree to hang around your neck,
said *a country is more important*

*than one person.* I don't know.
I've read emails of the new torture—
an overhead projector behind a prisoner,
turned on, until he feels his head

will catch fire. Last week, over baklava
and tea, rain pounding the door,
"Ashraf" spoke of barbed wire, boycotts
and curfews—how his dozen siblings split

into sides. *Israeli soldiers*
*hurt you, and we wanted them to hurt.*
*We couldn't imagine any other way.*
I wrote his story down. We met

again. He said I still didn't understand.
He said *write me out, keep only*
*the general outline, not how I slipped*
*through checkpoints or where I hid*

*when they came for us.* What I wrote or said,
each revealing detail, could spell
someone's end. When the story appeared
in the *Voice*, he only ghosted its margins, shadow

to a place not fully his. But there's no story
without particulars. What resistance could live
on the stale bread of statistics, the drought
of broken accords? It almost requires

bloodstained walls of a mosque,
prostrate backs shot through—a visible sign
of an invisible disgrace. Today, I open
the newspaper, try to peer between the grain

of a photo: a staggering crowd, arms entwined
and straining, as if to hold something back.
It could be us, facing a danger constantly
off-screen. No, we were born here.

On the stove, potatoes boil.
NPR segues labor strike
and missile strike with witty violin.
Twilight, I'm looking out the window,

trying to strike a few words
into flame. The dark lowers its wet sack,
then hoods the whole house. Outside,
something is falling. I strain to see it

past the glare of the kitchen light.

Abdal Rahman Mozayen, *Beautiful Women of Palestine: Hope and Return*, 1986.
Oil on canvas, 31.5″ × 24″

Fawzia Afzal-Khan

## In Memoriam: Edward Said 1935-2003


I cried for the man in the
cashmere coat
i cried for the boy from
palestine
i cried for my hero-worship-shivering
with delight
at the name mispronounced
a little bit new
a little bit not

recognition is a luxury we
never realized till we saw
 its haunting
absence
hovering around the postcolonial
figure he cut dashingly
gaunt as the hunger artist
 he had become

in his not-so-late
years the hunger you say
was always there
cashmere coat
and all
 a hunger for somewhere
Other

i cried for the critic
for his text
for the world
when i read his piano would
no longer make bold
 pleas for a peace
turning into a luxury
we may not recognize

when the world goes
sane
with that smile
in the coat

Abdal Rahman Mozayen, *Birth of the Intifada*, 1989. Ink on paper, 21˝ × 16˝

Deema Shehabi

**At the Dome of the Rock**

Jerusalem in the afternoon is the bitterness of two hundred
winter-bare olive trees fallen in the distance. Jerusalem
in the soft afternoon is a woman sitting at the edge of the Mosque
with her dried-up knees tucked beneath her, listening to shipwrecks
of holy words. If you sit beside her under the stone arch facing the Old
City, beneath the lacquered air that hooks into every crevice of skin,
your blood will unleash with her dreams, the Dome
will undulate gold, and her exhausted scars
will gleam across her overly kissed forehead.
She will ask you to come closer, and when you do,
She will lift the sea of her arms from the furls of her chest
and say: *this is the dim sky I have loved ever since I was a child.*

Jumana Husseini, *Sabra and Shatila*, 1982. Collage, 31″ × 23″

D. H. Melhem

**Those Policemen Are Sleeping:**
**A Call to the Children of Israel and Palestine**

*Caption: Four Palestinian police officers lie dead in a Ramallah office building, Saturday, March 30, 2002. The five bodies (one not pictured) all with gunshot wounds to the head, were laying in a dark hallway where the walls were splattered with blood and bullet holes. (AP Photo/Nasser Nasser)*

Those policemen are sleeping. They lie,
five in a doorway, each one neatly shot in the head,
huddled like derelicts. In the dereliction of death, they cannot guard
Ramallah, or Arafat, or anything or anyone.
They cannot guard children or mothers or old men.
Their blood, no longer confined, dances freely out the doorway
toward blasted olive groves and rubble of bulldozed homes
and shows its sad triumph in the street:
*We are fathers, lovers, people like yourselves!* it cries.

A few miles away Israeli children are sleeping. Dead in holiday clothes.
A Palestinian boy in pieces among them. They are all sleeping,
sleeping, all belong to one signature. They don't need identification
cards, or passports. They don't need to sign in or sign up.
God/Allah/Jehovah welcomes them. It's like a festival in heaven.
Pesach and Easter, cakes and goodies and traditional sayings,
chanting and singing and hard-boiled eggs,
bitter herbs and date cakes. All the shades sharing one earth,
a single territory, the air sweet above them, the sky a heavenly blue,
while the music of the spheres, like bells of sunlight,
chimes each flight into heaven.

War keeps taking, taking
sucks marrow,
marries the dead to the dead
and the living to the dead.
War is insatiable,
it has a stomach for youth
the delectable sweetness of babies
it spits out old people
it spares lives as lottery prizes.

And faith? What of faith?
I have faith in sunlight, in moonlight,

in a dandelion that gives its bitter food
and plain beauty,
in a smile, in the smell of soap,
in a page turned slowly,
faith in the Jesus of Peace, the Muhammad of Peace,
the Moses of Peace, the Buddha of Peace,
I have faith in the possible footsteps
of Gandhi and King.

What Moloch is this who beckons Israel?
And beckons Palestine?
Or is it a brave ancestor who fought vainly,
who summons you to his fate?
Is the world better off
for the killing?

Cure yourselves of the past.
It loves only itself.
Its plagues of grief and vengeance
that heavily armor the heart
and seemingly coat it with mail
can be as light as a shroud
or a mirage
in your vision.

Another world is possible.

Lisa Suhair Majaj

**This is Not a Massacre**

*What kind of war is this?*
*—Amira Hass, Ha'aretz, April 19, 2002*

This is a humanitarian operation.
All efforts have been made to protect
civilians. Homes demolished
above the heads of owners
ensure the absence of booby-traps.
Surely the dead are grateful:
this operation saved lives.

Our task is damage control.
Keep out the medical teams.
Let the voices beneath the rubble
fade away. Keep out the Red Cross,
the ambulances, the international observers,
the civilians bearing food and water:
mercy has no place
in the "city of bombers."

Extermination of vipers' nests
requires absolute precision.
Ignore the survivors
searching through ruins for shards
of their lives: a plate, a shoe,
a cup, a sack of rice. Ignore
the strewn body parts,
the leg twisted yards away
from the white and bloated hand;
the boys cradling a small charred foot.
Dismembered bodies
cannot remember themselves.

What remains? Only traces.
That photo (dead girl,
hand clutched at her side,
once-white ribbon still discernible
on her pallid profile,
ashen skin melting into the dust
that clogs her mouth):

nothing more than shadow
of the drowned, odor of mint
wafting from a grave.

Say it fast over and over:
this is not a massacre this
is not a massacre this is not
a massacre this is not a
massacre this is not
a massacre this is not a
massacre

*for the people of Jenin, Palestine*

Pierre Joris

## 23 isolation (infirad)

I'm infuriated
by isolation

but it is the only I
there is under

the sun its wheel
rolls out of

infrared ultra
violent blue

of son's stroke
post isolation

post to stand
there on a corner

of the desert this
life wants to

make of
us all

unfinished by
isolation

an I in
iso elation

plays with itself
hands in pockets

it stands, not
yet an endangered

species, an endangering
isolato Americano

on the corner

of any desert-

ed street between
here & here

the pocket billiards
of empire an isolation

Muhammad Rakoui, *Prisoner*, 1984. Dry ink, pastel, and wax crayon on cloth, 14″ × 10″

Nizar Wattad (a.k.a. Ragtop)

**Free the P**


I place my palms to the East
Where my people seek peace
And freedom from police control, checkpoints and patrols
Domination from another nation
We used to be brothers like Cain
Now they got us living under occupation the pain
Is just a feeling I can't possibly explain
But the population of Palestine could probably paint
A proper picture of their predicament to publish and frame

Put it down for posterity's sake:
Free the P

Which stands for free the Public from the Prejudices
That Pop culture Places in your Psyche Permanently
Propaganda from the President to media Pundits
To Preachers Preaching on the TV 'bout the People who done it
Politicians getting Paid to Put People in Prison
For Puffing Pot and just building
Something different from what they live in the vision
Is not to give in but to just give 'em hell
Impel Proactive change with the thoughts I Propel—
Free the P?
That's for anybody trapped in a jail
That should be free instead of breathing stale air in a cell
For every Parent that to Protect their child would spark heat?
Free the P is for the women living in this Patriarchy
And for all the artists
That do this shit from the heart:
From the West Bank to the West Coast we start
To connect and get close, Professin' our best hopes—
Despite the stress blessed 'cause it's something in our chest
That Love—

Fathi Ghaban, *Torture at Ansar Prison*, 1984. Ink on paper, 14″ × 9″

Mahmoud Darwish

## Another Day Will Come

Another day will come, a womanly day
diaphanous in metaphor, complete in being,
diamond and processional in visitation, sunny,
flexible, with a light shadow. No one will feel
a desire for suicide or for leaving. All
things, outside the past, natural and real,
will be synonyms of their early traits. As if time
is slumbering on vacation…"Extend your lovely
beauty-time. Sunbathe in the sun of your silken breasts,
and wait until good omen arrives. Later
we will grow older. We have enough time
to grow older after this day…" /
Another day will come, a womanly day
song like in gesture, lapis in greeting
and in phrase. All things will be feminine outside
the past. Water will flow from rock's bosom.
No dust, no drought, no defeat.
And a dove will sleep in the afternoon in an abandoned
combat tank if it doesn't find a small nest
in the lovers' bed…

*Translated from the Arabic by Fady Joudah*

Marilyn Hacker

**Morning News**

Spring wafts up the smell of bus exhaust, of bread
and fried potatoes, tips green on the branches,
repeats old news: arrogance, ignorance, war.
A cinder-block wall shared by two houses
is new rubble. On one side was a kitchen
sink and a cupboard, on the other was
a bed, a bookshelf, three framed photographs.

Glass is shattered across the photographs;
two half-circles of hardened pocket-bread
sit on the cupboard. There provisionally was
shelter, a plastic truck under the branches
of a fig-tree. A knife flashed in the kitchen,
merely dicing garlic. Engines of war
move inexorably towards certain houses

while citizens sit safe in other houses
reading the newspaper, whose photographs
make sanitized excuses for the war.
There are innumerable kinds of bread
brought up from bakeries, baked in the kitchen:
the date, the latitude, tell which one was
dropped by a child beneath the bloodied branches.

The uncontrolled and multifurcate branches
of possibility infiltrate houses'
walls, windowframes, ceilings. Where there was
a tower, a town: ash and burnt wires, a graph
on a distant computer screen. Elsewhere, a kitchen
table's setting gapes, where children bred
to branch into new lives were culled for war.

Who wore this starched smocked cotton dress? Who wore
this jersey blazoned for the local branch
of the district soccer team? Who left this black bread
and this flat gold bread in their abandoned houses?
Whose father begged for mercy in the kitchen?
Whose memory will frame the photograph
and use the memory for what it was

never meant for by this girl, that old man, who was
caught on a ball-field, near a window: war,
exhorted through the grief a photograph
revives. (Or was the team a covert branch
of a banned group; were maps drawn in the kitchen,
a bomb thrust in a hollowed loaf of bread?)
What did the old men pray for in their houses

of prayer, the teachers teach in schoolhouses
between blackouts and blasts, when each word was
flensed by new censure, books exchanged for bread,
both hostage to the happenstance of war?
Sometimes the only schoolroom is a kitchen.
Outside the window, black strokes on a graph
of broken glass, birds line up on bare branches.

"This letter curves, this one spreads its branches
like friends holding hands outside their houses."
Was the lesson stopped by gunfire? Was
there panic, silence? Does a torn photograph
still gather children in the teacher's kitchen?
Are they there meticulously learning war-
time lessons with the signs for house, book, bread?

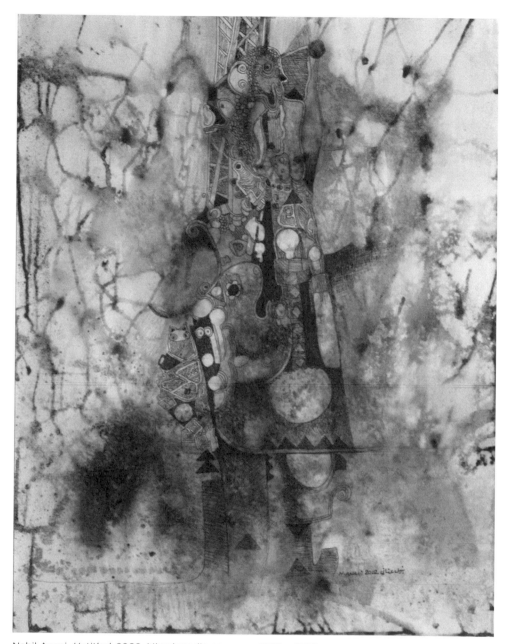

Nabil Anani, *Untitled*, 2002. Mixed media on paper, 27.5″ × 19.5″

Suheir Hammad

## break (bas)


bas
bastana
ana bastana
bas

daily papers photo babies
charred bread no life

venus chaired motionless shaking
bleeds currents

astonished stars cry

bas

gather armless
gather heart broke
gather just broke
gather harvest
gather blood
gather thirst

ride moon bare
back through night
conjure lion stretch
sunrise reaching raw ankles

bas ana

image mirage libnan woman khadra
khalas last call rouged up bought
down maze mezze liquor
rich sweat raw flesh mint civil
warm family foreign faded
coast defiant jaded
jupiter altar smote cypress
loudest crescent siren

occupier vampire
tell like is

gather orphaned
gather barren
gather limbs
gather touch
gather eye light
gather close
realize

bastana ana

alone
bas not

Alicia Ostriker

**Baby Carriages**

In the photograph there are two of them, and a stroller.
The women sit on a bench, wearing their usual day clothes,
That thin stooped one wears a flowered rayon dress,

This one has dark lipstick on, a third is older and has a perm.
The women look relaxed, like people who have known each other forever.
Later they'll feed their babies, then do the laundry or go shopping.

I don't see the babies but I feel their presence
Like invisible magnets that keep the photograph from falling apart,
The animal premise of the whole image.

Behind the bench is a strip of garden and a brick wall
The shadowless sun is bathing. The carriages themselves are funny,
High off the ground and shaped and lacquered like the coaches of royalty.

The date of the photograph is 1942. Wartime, the home front,
It makes sense, I stand in front of it on the museum wall
For a long time, thinking: Here's the real story. If only.

Naomi Shihab Nye

**Kindness**


Before you know what kindness really is
you must lose things,
feel the future dissolve in a moment
like salt in a weakened broth.
What you held in your hand,
what you counted and carefully saved,
all this must go so you know
how desolate the landscape can be
between the regions of kindness.
How you ride and ride
thinking the bus will never stop,
the passengers eating maize and chicken
will stare out the window forever.

Before you learn the tender gravity of kindness,
you must travel where the Indian in a white poncho
lies dead by the side of the road.
You must see how this could be you,
how he too was someone
who journeyed through the night with plans
and the simple breath that kept him alive.

Before you know kindness as the deepest thing inside,
you must know sorrow as the other deepest thing.
You must wake up with sorrow.
You must speak to it till your voice
catches the thread of all sorrows
and you see the size of the cloth.

Then it is only kindness that makes sense anymore,
only kindness that ties your shoes
and sends you out into the day to mail letters and purchase bread,
only kindness that raises its head
from the crowd of the world to say
It is I you have been looking for,
and then goes with you everywhere
like a shadow or a friend.

Jawad Ibrahim, FROM Between Bullets and Stones, 2000. Ink wash on paper, 11.5˝ × 8.25˝

Fady Joudah

**An Idea of Return**


I look for your hair and find it
In the night, holding color,
Amber copper,
After so many years inside an envelope.

And I think of the soul
Making speeches hours ago:

The carpenter
Dying of cancer in a hospital bed
Saying, god, I know
You've given me misfortune

But when I get up there
There'd better be a damn
Good reason for it,
I've got nothing against trees.

The carpenter thought I was kind
And searched my nametag for a while

Then said: I know your people.
They're good people, they
Have suffered enough,
And the city is theirs—

The carpenter would be dead by morning.
And why

Did I think your hair
Would have turned white by now?
Like the Mediterranean, frothing at the shore.
And why

You asked for your hair back
Is why I kept it:

Like the city that is only mine
When I'm confused for another.

Suleiman Mansour, *Our Fathers and Grandfathers*, 1974. Oil on canvas, 25″ × 23″

Annemarie Jacir

**changing names**


at night they dream
in beds that don't belong to them
in houses
built by ghosts
in triumphant villages
that have extinguished others

beit jibrin becomes beyt guvrin
salama disappears
girls roller skate in
a tel aviv suburb
um khalid engulfed into netanya
a man spreads a beach umbrella

qisarya lands become sedot yam
the village mosque converted into a bar
in others...
           *three houses, two shrines and a school remain*
overgrown in cactus
           weeds

a history
           they claim not to know

they dream
in this country
in summer
                in song
                          spirit
                                 land

at night...listen
after the cars stop rushing past
the neighbors voices have peeled away
and the screech of buses and garbage trucks less frequent

silence

a soundless hum
unrelenting

constant
an insomniac stirs

wind scratches at the windows
underneath,
the floor seems to rise
an audible silence
deafens
encroaches

this is the sound of bir salim
al mukhayzin
saydun
of erased villages
buried in stones and memories

of children awakening in the night

they choose a night
so dark
the line between the shore and the land
is indiscernible

waves encroach
circle the earth like dogs
the children of samra
nimrin
tabsur
awake others

they hold fire
eat black clouds
tear thunder

a letter arrives

       *beware the wrath of the*
       *unborn children of palestine*

at night, others dream
at the front door, roller skates wait for morning
a breakfast table has been set

and under the floorboards
in darkness

children push
rise

they know this:
abu dis is just

    abu dis

Vera Tamari, *Tree Poem I*, 2006. Mixed media collage, 11.5″ × 15.5″

Nathalie Handal

## Abu Jamal's Olive Trees

He works the soil
Day after day
He hasn't known peace
His entire life
He hasn't had dreams
He believes possible
He considers death and life at every instinct
He tells his wife
To remind him what he looks like—
His eyes empty now
His gut cold
His olive trees uprooted.
And then he says with a smile:
I would love to know the names
Of those who will pick olives
On our land in October...
*What trees* she asks:
　　*The one growing.*

Dima Hilal

## A Tree in Rafah

*for Rachel Corrie*

Sprinkle her with rose water
And crushed gardenias

Overturn the earth
With your hands

Lower her gently
Gently
Into the ground

This child
This daughter
Belongs to us

A bullhorn,
Her only weapon

Resistance,
Her body

Remember Rosa Parks,
Tiananmen Square,
Rachel

No greater sacrifice
No greater sacrifice
Than this

Now the word *ache*
Weighs down the middle of her name
Our loss lodged in our throats

We look for Rachel
Beneath a tree in Rafah

Bending over her journal
What would she have written next?

Whose stories will remain untold?

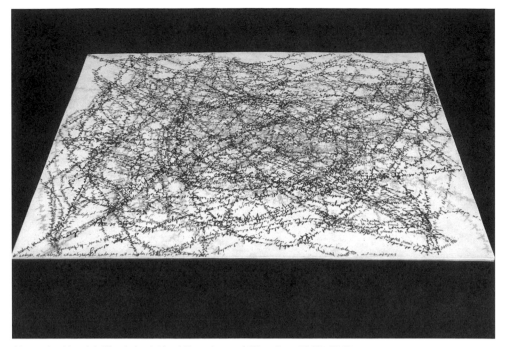

Alexandra Handal, *The Labyrinth of Remains and Migration*, 2000–2001.
Vellum, pencil, and Plexiglass, dimensions variable

*Our creativity binds us together,*

*our vision catapults us forward,*

*we may suffer setbacks,*

*but our horizon is near.*

Rajie Cook, *Epitaph for a Roadmap*, 2006. Digital print on paper construction, 24″ × 27.5″

# About the Poets

**Fawzia Afzal-Khan** is professor of English at Montclair University. She is the editor of *Shattering Stereotypes: Muslim Women Speak Out* (Interlink Books, 2005). Her scholarly articles have appeared in numerous journals, including the *Journal of South Asian Studies*, *NWSA Journal*, *Social Text*, *Womanist Theory and Research*, and *Wasafiri*. Among her other scholarly recognitions, Professor Afzal-Khan has been awarded a W.E.B. Dubois Fellowship and a grant from the American Institute of Pakistan Studies.

**Amiri Baraka** is a poet, critic, and political activist. He is the author of numerous volumes of poetry, including *Selected Poetry of Amiri Baraka/LeRoi Jones* (William Morrow & Co, 1979), *The Music: Reflections on Jazz and Blues* (William Morrow & Co, 1987), and *Somebody Blew Up America & Other Poems* (House of Nehesi Publishers, 2003). Among his many awards and honors are an Obie, the American Academy of Arts & Letters award, the James Weldon Johnson Medal for contributions to the arts, and grants from the Rockefeller Foundation and the National Endowment for the Arts.

**Ibtisam Barakat** is the author of *Tasting the Sky: A Palestinian Childhood* (Farrar, Straus and Giroux, 2007). She grew up in Ramallah and currently resides in the United States. Her work centers on healing social injustices, especially in the lives of young people. She has taught language ethics at Stephens College in Columbia, Missouri and is the founder of Write Your Life seminars.

**Hamida Begum**, who is ten years old, is a student at Muwatta Weekend Maktab, an Islamic educational institute based in London, England. She enjoys creative handicraft as a hobby and hopes to someday work toward portraying a more accurate and clear image of Islam and Muslims.

**Omar Chakaki** was born in the Middle East to a Syrian family and emigrated to the United States at age four. He was raised in the Washington, D.C. area and earned a B.A. in Architecture/Digital Art from the University of Virginia in 2003. Chakaki currently resides in Los Angeles, where his role as Omar Offendum (of the bi-coastal hip-hop group the N.O.M.A.D.S.) has given him the opportunity to perform at venues across the globe, from the House of Blues in Hollywood to the Citadel in Amman, Jordan.

**Hayan Charara** is an Arab-American poet and the editor of the forthcoming anthology *Inclined to Speak: An Anthology of Contemporary Arab-American Poetry* (University of Arkansas Press, 2008). He has authored two books of poetry, *The Alchemist's Diary* (Hanging Loose Press, 2001) and *The Sadness of Others* (Carnegie Mellon University Press, 2006). His poetry has appeared in numerous literary journals and anthologies, including the *Birmingham Poetry Review*, *Cream City Review*, *Arab Detroit: From Margin to Mainstream* (Wayne State University Press, 2000), and *Present Tense: Poets in the World* (Hanging Loose Press, 2005).

**Mahmoud Darwish** is the author of more than thirty books of poetry and prose. He has received numerous international awards, including the Knight of the Order of Arts and Letters, the Lannan Foundation Prize for Cultural Freedom, and the Prince Claus Prize. His most recent collection of work translated to English is *The Butterfly's Burden* (Copper Canyon Press, 2006).

**Kathy Engel** is a poet, teacher, producer, and strategic planner for peace and social justice organizations. She is the author of two collections of poetry, *Banish the Tentative* (Wingding and Honey Press, 1989) and *Ruth's Skirts* (IKON, 2007). She is the co-editor of *We Begin Here: Poems for Palestine and Lebanon* (Interlink Books, 2007). Engel currently serves on the advisory board of the United States Campaign to End the Israeli Occupation.

**Veronica Golos** is the author of *A Bell Buried Deep* (Story Line Press, 2003). A recipient of the Nicholas Roerich Poetry Prize, Golos' work has appeared in *Rattapallax*, *Poetry London*, *Oberon*, *Zeek*, *Heliotrope*, *Tribes*, *Long Shot*, *Bridges*, and *Drunken Boat*. She is a founding member of 3poets4peace, a performance group that donates proceeds from its work to peace organizations. Golos was nominated as the Best Spoken Word Artist at the 2006 Just Plain Folks American Music Awards. She resides in Taos, New Mexico.

**Marilyn Hacker** is the author of several collections of poems, including *Desesperanto: Poems 1999-2002* (W. W. Norton & Company, 2003) and *Presentation Piece* (Viking Press, 1974), which was the Lamont Poetry Selection of the Academy of American Poets and a National Book Award winner. She also translated Vénus Khoury-Ghata's poetry, published in *Here There Was Once a Country* (Oberlin College Press, 2001) and *She Says* (Graywolf Press, 2003). Hacker has received numerous honors, including the Bernard F. Conners Prize from the *Paris Review* and fellowships from the Guggenheim Foundation and the Ingram Merrill Foundation.

**Marian Haddad** was born and raised in El Paso, Texas. She is the author of *Somewhere Between Mexico and a River Called Home* (Pecan Grove Press, 2004). Her poetry and essays have been featured in numerous magazines and journals, including the *Rio Grande Review*, *Texas Observer*, and *Sin Fronteras/Writers Without Borders*. She was a recipient of a National Endowment for the Humanities Fellowship to study philosophy at the University of Notre Dame. She currently lives in San Antonio, where she works as a lecturer, freelance writer, manuscript consultant, and visiting writer.

**Laila Halaby** was born in Lebanon to a Jordanian father and American mother, and raised in the United States. She is the author of the novels *West of the Jordan* (Beacon Press, 2003) and *Once in a Promised Land* (Beacon Press, 2007). Her poetry has been featured in numerous anthologies, including *The Poetry of Arab Women: A Contemporary Anthology* (Interlink Books, 2000), and *The Flag of Childhood: Poems From the Middle East* (Aladdin, 2002). She currently lives in Tucson, Arizona.

**Suheir Hammad** is the author of *Born Palestinian, Born Black* (Writers & Readers

Publishing, 1996), *Drops of This Story* (Writers & Readers Publishing, 1996), and *ZaatarDiva* (Rattapallax Press, 2006). Reared in Brooklyn by Palestinian refugee parents, she has traveled around the world reading her poetry. A winner of numerous writing awards, she is a writer and cast member of the TONY Award-winning *Def Poetry Jam* on Broadway.

**Nathalie Handal** is the author of *The Neverfield* (Interlink Books, 2005) and *The Lives of Rain* (Interlink Books, 2005), which was shortlisted for the Agnes Lynch Starrett Poetry Prize/the Pitt Poetry Series. She has recorded two CDs of poetry, *Traveling Rooms* (1999) and *Spell* (2006). She is the editor of *The Poetry of Arab Women: A Contemporary Anthology* (Interlink Books, 2000), a winner of the Pen Oakland/ Josephine Miles Award and an Academy of American Poets bestseller, and the co-editor of the forthcoming anthology, *Language for a New Century: Contemporary Poetry from the Middle East, Asia & Beyond* (W.W. Norton & Co, 2008).

**Dima Hilal** was born in Beirut and raised in California. Her poetry and writing has appeared in numerous journals, anthologies, and newspapers, including the *San Francisco Chronicle*, *Orion*, *Aramco*, *The Poetry of Arab Women: A Contemporary Anthology* (Interlink Books, 2001), and *Scheherazade's Legacy: Arab and Arab-American Women on Writing* (Praeger, 2004). Her libretto, *Raheel*, was a finalist in the Oakland East Bay Symphony's Words and Music Project. She is currently working on a collection of poetry.

**Melissa Hotchkiss** is a poet and editor. Her first book of poems, *Storm Damage*, was published by Tupelo Press in 2002. Her work has appeared in the *Marlboro Review*, *Four Way Reader #2*, *New York Times*, *Free Inquiry*, *LIT*, *7 Carmine*, *Cortland Review*, *3rd bed*, *Gathering of the Tribes*, *Lyric Poetry Review*, *Upstairs at Duroc*, *Diner*, and *Heliotrope*. Her prose has appeared in the *New York Times* and *New Virginia Review*. Hotchkiss is an editor of the poetry journal *Barrow Street*. She lives in New York City with her dog, Jesse.

**Annemarie Jacir** is a Palestinian filmmaker, poet, and activist based in Ramallah. Selected for the Sundance Filmmaker's Lab in Utah and awarded several screenwriting awards, Jacir focuses on issues of race, class, and liberation. She has read with poet Amiri Baraka, and her work has been published in numerous literary journals and anthologies, including the *Crab Orchard Review* and *The Poetry of Arab Women: A Contemporary Anthology* (Interlink Books, 2001).

**Pierre Joris** has published over twenty books and chapbooks of poetry, including *Breccia* (Guernica Editions, 1987), *Turbulence* (Saint Lazaire Press, 1991), and *Poasis: Selected Poems* 1986-1999 (Wesleyan University Press, 2001). He co-edited the two-volume anthology of poetry, *Poems for the Millennium: The University of California Book of Modern & Postmodern Poetry* (University of California Press, 1998) and, in 2003, under the title of A Nomad Poetics, published a selection of essays.

**Fady Joudah** is a physician, member of Doctors Without Borders, translator, and poet. He is also the poetry editor of RAWI (Radius of Arab American Writers). His poetry has appeared in various journals, including the *Iowa Review*, *Kenyon Review*, *Prairie Schooner*, and *Beloit Poetry Journal*. His translation of Mahmoud Darwish's recent works is collected in *The Butterfly's Burden*, published by Copper Canyon Press (2007).

**Remi Kanazi** is a Palestinian-American poet and writer based in New York City. He is the co-founder of the political website PoeticInjustice.net. His political commentary, which primarily focuses on Palestine, has been featured in numerous print and online publications. He recently appeared in the New York Arab American Comedy Festival and has been regularly featured on the Al Jazeera English program the *Listening Post*.

**Vénus Khoury-Ghata** was born in northern Lebanon. She is a poet and novelist and has written fourteen novels and twelve collections of poetry in French. She has two collections of poetry translated into English, *Here There Was Once a Country* (Oberlin College Press, 2001) and *She Says* (Graywolf Press, 2003). Her work has been translated into several languages, including English, Arabic, Italian, Russian, and Polish.

**Lisa Suhair Majaj** is a Palestinian-American. Her creative work has been published in over fifty journals and anthologies in the United States and abroad. Her scholarly work focuses on Arab-American literature, and she has co-edited three collections of critical essays: *Going Global: The Transnational Reception of Third World Women Writers* (Routledge, 2000), *Etel Adnan: Critical Essays on the Arab-American Writer and Artist* (McFarland & Company, 2002), and *Intersections: Gender, Nation and Community in Arab Women's Novels* (Syracuse University Press, 2002). She lives in Nicosia, Cyprus.

**D. H. Melhem** is the author of seven books of poetry, three novels, a musical drama, a creative writing workbook, over sixty essays, and two edited anthologies. Her critical works on black poets include the first comprehensive study of Gwendolyn Brooks. Among her many awards for poetry and prose are an American Book Award, a National Endowment for the Humanities Fellowship, three Pushcart Prize nominations, and a CUNY Ph.D. Alumni Association Special Achievement Award. She is the winner of the 2007 RAWI Lifetime Achievement Award. Dr. Melhem also serves as vice-president of the International Women's Writing Guild.

**Philip Metres** is a poet and a translator whose work has appeared in numerous journals and in *Best American Poetry* (Scribner, 2002). His books include *A Kindred Orphanhood: Selected Poems of Sergey Gandlevsky* (Zephyr Press, 2003), *Primer for Non-Native Speakers* (Kent State University Press, 2004), *Catalogue of Comedic Novelties: Selected Poems of Lev Rubinstein* (Ugly Duckling Presse, 2004), *Instants* (Ugly Duckling Presse, 2006), and *Behind the Lines: War Resistance Poetry on the American Homefront, Since 1941* (University of Iowa Press, 2007). He teaches literature and creative writing at John Carroll University in Cleveland, Ohio.

**E. Ethelbert Miller** is the author of several collections of poetry, including *How We Sleep on the Nights We Don't Make Love* (Curbstone Press, 2004). He is also the editor of numerous anthologies, including *In Search of Color Everywhere: A Collection of*

*African-American Poetry* (Stewart, Tabori & Chang, 1994), which received the PEN Oakland Josephine Miles Award. Miller has received a number of other awards and honors, including an O.B. Hardison, Jr. Poetry Prize and the Stephen Henderson Poetry Award from the African-American Literature and Culture Society.

**J. A. Miller** is a grandmother and activist. She lived in the Middle East for many years, where she learned to speak fluent Arabic. She has published online essays at *Dissident Voice, State of Nature*, and *Counterpunch* as well Burma Shave-style doggerel at PoeticInjustice.net. Miller, a systems analyst by day, likes nothing better than to have a bit of poetic fun with the legion of western progressives besotted with Zionism. She is currently working on a book about the Protestant origins of the Zionist project.

**Mr. Tibbz** is a Sudanese conceived/D.C.-born/Virginia-bred hip-hop artist. Raised all over the map—from the madness of Dodge City in the mid-80's, the war drenched Sudan in the late 80's, recently independent Namibia in the 90's, the English countryside in '91, and frequent stops to Apartheid and post-Apartheid South Africa—he got to see a lot of what most choose to deny or try to hide about the ugly system we live in. Also known as Da Dirty Cousin for his obsessive vulgarity, he tears through issues ranging from suicide bombings to selling weed in his underwear.

**Naomi Shihab Nye** is a Palestinian-American poet. Her books of poems include *Hugging the Jukebox* (Breitenbush Books, 1982), *Red Suitcase* (BOA Editions, 1994), *Fuel* (BOA Editions, 1998), *19 Varieties of Gazelle: Poems of the Middle East* (Greenwillow, 2002), and *You and Yours* (BOA Editions, 2005). Nye has received numerous awards, including the Academy of American Poets' Lavan Award and four Pushcart Prizes. She has been a Lannan Fellow, a Guggenheim Fellow, and a Wittner Bynner Fellow. She currently lives in San Antonio, Texas.

**Alicia Ostriker** is an American poet and critic. She has authored eleven books of poetry. Her poetry has been featured in the *New Yorker, Paris Review, Antaeus, Nation, Poetry, American Poetry Review, Kenyon Review, Atlantic, MS, Tikkun*, and many other journals and anthologies. The recipient of numerous honors, she has received awards from the National Endowment for the Arts, the Poetry Society of America, the San Francisco State Poetry Center, the Judah Magnes Museum, the New Jersey Arts Council, the Rockefeller Foundation, and the Guggenheim Foundation. She is Professor Emerita of English at Rutgers University.

**Tahani Salah** is a performer, poet, and activist in Brooklyn. For the last five years, she has worked with Urban Word NYC, a youth spoken word collective in New York City. She was a 2006 Urban Word NYC slam team member, serves as the Youth Outreach Coordinator, and sits on the Urban Word Youth board. As a Palestinian-American Muslim woman, she is committed to bringing light and solutions to problems faced by people from communities whose voices are silenced. She is currently working on her first collection of poetry.

**Junichi P. Semitsu** is a professor at the University of San Diego School of Law, a blogger for Poplicks.com, and a poet. While teaching at the University of California, Berkeley, he was the director of June Jordan's Poetry for the People. His work has appeared in numerous publications, including the *Stanford Law Review*, *Chicago Tribune*, and *New Crisis*. He was a finalist in the San Francisco Poetry Slam and has performed on National Public Radio.

**Deema Shehabi** is a Palestinian poet who grew up in the Arab world. Her poems have appeared in various anthologies and journals, including the *Atlanta Review*, *Bat City Review*, *Crab Orchard*, *Kenyon Review*, *Mississippi Review*, *Drunken Boat*, *DMQ Review*, *Flyway*, *Body Eclectic*, *White Ink*, and *The Poetry of Arab Women: A Contemporary Anthology* (Interlink Books, 2000). She has been nominated for a Pushcart Prize and her poems have been translated into French and Farsi. She resides in California with her husband and two sons.

**Patricia Smith** is the author of four books of poetry, including *Teahouse of the Almighty* (Coffee House Press, 2006), a 2005 National Poetry Series selection. She is a 2007 winner of the Chautauqua Literary Journal Award in Poetry and the Paterson Poetry Prize. A four-time individual champion on the National Poetry Slam, Smith has also been a featured poet on HBO's *Def Poetry Jam*. She has served as the Bruce McEver Chair in Writing at Georgia Tech University and is a faculty member of Cave Canem, an organization dedicated to the uncovering and nurturing of new voices in African-American poetry.

**Melissa Tuckey** is a poet, activist, and teacher living in Washington, D.C. Her poems have been published in numerous journals, including *Beloit Poetry Journal*, *Poet Lore*, *Southeast Review*, among others. She is an Ohio Arts Council Grant recipient. She teaches writing at George Mason University and serves as Events Coordinator for D.C. Poets Against the War. Her chapbook, *Rope As Witness*, has been recently published and released by Pudding House Press.

**Nizar Wattad** (a.k.a. Ragtop) was born in Palestine and raised in Tennessee. He is a Palestinian-American hip-hop artist and screenwriter. He earned his undergraduate degree from the George Washington University in 2001, and has since written and edited for several literary and news publications. Wattad earned an M.A. in screenwriting from the University of Southern California in 2006, and his thesis screenplay, *Agency*, was a semi-finalist in that year's Final Draft Big Break, Brass Brad Mentorship, and ABC/Walt Disney Company Writing Fellowship competitions.

**Sholeh Wolpé** was born in Iran. She is the author of *The Scar Saloon* (Red Hen Press, 2004), *Sin—Poems of Forugh Farrokhzad* (University of Arkansas Press, 2007), and *Rooftops of Tehran* (Red Hen Press, 2008). Her poems, translations, essays, and reviews have appeared in scores of literary journals, periodicals, and anthologies worldwide, and have been translated into several languages. She lives in Los Angeles.

**Ghassan Zaqtan** was born in the Palestinian Diaspora and currently resides in Ramallah.

He has authored numerous volumes of poetry. His novel, *Describing the Past*, was published in Jordan in 1995. Zaqtan is the editor of the poetry quarterly, *Al-Shou'ara*, the editor of the literary page of *Al-Ayyam*, and the co-founder and director of the House of Poetry in Ramallah. He currently works at the Palestinian Ministry of Culture.

# Works Cited

**Fawzia Afzal-Khan**, "In Memoriam: Edward Said 1935-2003." Reprinted by permission of author.

**Amiri Baraka**, "Enemy of Civilization." Reprinted by permission of author.

**Ibtisam Barakat**, "Curfew," first appeared on UniVerseofPoetry.org. Reprinted by permission of author. "War Layers." Reprinted by permission of author.

**Hamida Begum**, "The Promised Land." Printed by permission of author.

**Hayan Charara**, "Hamza Aweiwi, a Shoemaker in Hebron," from *The Alchemist's Diary* (Hanging Loose Press, 2001). Reprinted by permission of author. "Price of Tomatoes." Reprinted by permission of author.

**Mahmoud Darwish**, "Who Am I, Without Exile?" and "Another Day Will Come," translated by Fady Joudah. Reprinted by permission of translator.

**Kathy Engel**, "Untitled." Reprinted by permission of author.

**Veronica Golos**, "Cain." Reprinted by permission of author.

**Marilyn Hacker**, "Morning News," from *Desesperanto: Poems 1999-2002* (W. W. Norton & Company, 2003). Reprinted by permission of author.

**Marian Haddad**, "Making Arabic Coffee." Reprinted by permission of author.

**Laila Halaby**, "a moonlit visit." Printed by permission of author.

**Suheir Hammad**, "break (bas)." Printed by permission of author.

**Nathalie Handal**, "A Wall Against Our Breath" and "Abu Jamal's Olive Trees." Reprinted by permission of author.

**Dima Hilal**, "A Tree in Rafah" and "Ar-Rahman Road." Reprinted by permission of author.

**Melissa Hotchkiss**, "Regret." Reprinted by permission of author.

**Annemarie Jacir**, "changing names." Reprinted by permission of author.

**Pierre Joris**, "23 isolation (infirad)," from *Meditations on the Stations of Mansour*

*Al-Hallaj* (Anchorite Press, 2007). Reprinted by permission of author.

**Fady Joudah**, "An Idea of Return" and "The Tea and Sage Poem." Reprinted by permission of author.

**Remi Kanazi**, "Palestinian Identity." Printed by permission of author.

**Vénus Khoury-Ghata**, "The Seven Honeysuckle-sprigs of Wisdom," from *There Was Once a Country* (Oberlin College Press, 2001), translated by Marilyn Hacker. Reprinted by permission of translator.

**Lisa Suhair Majaj**, "The Coffin Maker Speaks," from *World Literature Today 80.6* (2006). Reprinted by permission of author. "This is Not a Massacre," from *Dance the Guns to Silence: 100 Poems for Ken Saro-Wiwa*, Ed. Nii Ayikwie Parkes and Kadija Sesay (Flipped Eye Publishing, 2005). Reprinted by permission of author.

**D. H. Melhem**, "Those Policemen Are Sleeping: A Call to the Children of Israel and Palestine," first appeared on Poetz.com (2002). Reprinted by permission of author.

**Philip Metres**, "Installation/Occupation," from *Mizna 8.2* (2006). Reprinted by permission of author. "Letter to My Sister," from *Artful Dodge 44/45* (2004). Reprinted by permission of author.

**E. Ethelbert Miller**, "Fathers in Exile." Reprinted by permission of author.

**J. A. Miller**, "Saudi Israelia." Printed by permission of author.

**Naomi Shihab Nye**, "My Father and the Figtree," from *Different Ways to Pray* (Breitenbush Publications, 1980). Reprinted by permission of author. "Kindness," from *Different Ways to Pray* (Breitenbush Publications, 1980). Reprinted by permission of author.

**The N.O.M.A.D.S.**, "Moot." Printed by permission of authors.

**Alicia Ostriker**, "Baby Carriages," from *Feminist Studies 30.1* (2004). Reprinted by permission of author.

**Tahani Salah**, "Hate." Printed by permission of author.

**Junichi P. Semitsu**, "Palestine in Athens." Reprinted by permission of author.

**Deema Shehabi**, "Lights Across the Dead Sea," from *Drunken Boat 7* (2005). Reprinted by permission of author. "At the Dome of the Rock." Reprinted by permission of author.

**Patricia Smith**, "Humming When We Find Her." Reprinted by permission of author.

**Melissa Tuckey**, "The Wheel" and "Portrait of Mona Lisa in Palestine." Reprinted by permission of author.

**Nizar Wattad (a.k.a. Ragtop)**, "Free the P." Printed by permission of author.

**Sholeh Wolpé**, "And So It Goes…" and "Morning After the U.S. Invasion of Iraq." Reprinted by permission of author.

**Ghassan Zaqtan**, "The Camp Prostitute" and "Black Horses," translated by May Jayyusi and Alan Brownjohn. Reprinted by permission of translators.